My love life & other disasters

poems

Josa Keyes

KeyesInk

First published 2021 by KeyesInk
London UK

ISBN: 978-0-9931248-5-3 (print)
ISBN: 978-0-9931248-6-0 (digital)

My Love Life and Other Disasters is a creative work of poetry.

For the man who wasn't there

About Josa Keyes

Formerly known as Josa Young, Josa Keyes was born in Kent, England. She read English Literature at Newnham College, University of Cambridge. In 2019, she completed a Master's in Creative Writing at Brunel University London with distinction and won the Arts & Humanities Faculty Dissertation Prize. She has worked as a commissioning editor and features writer for *Vogue*, *Tatler*, the *Telegraph*, the *Times* and *Country Living*, among many other publications. She has a parallel career as a digital content designer for the government and for big brands such as Land Rover. Her first novel *One Apple Tasted* was published in 2009 by Elliot & Thompson. Her second, *Sail Upon the Land*, was longlisted for the Historical Novel Society prize 2015. She lives in London, where she has been performing her poetry since 2016 at a variety of venues, including the Society Club and Blacks Club, Soho, and the Book Club, Shoreditch. *My Love Life & Other Disasters* is her first poetry collection. She has three children, now all grown – raising them is the creative act of which she is most proud.

Twitter @JosaKeyes
www.josayoungauthor.com

Contents

Love in a time of coronavirus

If I knew that Love was coming over
I'd polish every surface in my house
I'd scatter Vanish powder 'cross the floor
And bend my back like Millet's gleaners to brush
It firmly into every tuft and fibre.

Henry Hoover's smiling face would no longer
Lurk beneath a heap of laundry done
But suck up all the signs of carelessness
From mats and fitted carpets, boards and tiles.

I'd crawl on bended knee along the skirting board
And take the Pledge to every single mote
Mr Sheen would get an unaccustomed outing
And bleach would whiten every porcelain bowl.

The crusts of London's stony-hearted water
Would be fizzed away with liberal Viakal
Using old toothbrushes, I'd fidget all the traces
Of grub and grime that human life attracts
From every groove and cranny in my hard-won home.

Then I'd bash the cushions into shape
Light candles, make quenelles, chill wine.

But there's no sign that Love is coming over
No breathless call or text, no poetry for me
And so I'll drift within my usual cloudscape
Of dust and dregs and hair and old tea leaves.

The care and management of unwanted gifts

I thought that I had given him my heart
Looking back you cannot give your heart
If it is not received, enfolded in a breast
Sheltered like a bird within its downy nest

In fact, my heart was hanging out to dry
Pickled in a sour liquor of laughter and regret
Uncared for, kicked beneath the sofa
Smirched with dust, diminished with neglect

If you give your heart please do so carefully
Make sure the hands are there to take it tenderly
From your grasp, and not to let it slip
At once into the cold and unforgiving ashes
Of burnt out lust, and love that never was.

Exorcism for young ladies troubled by ghosts

The best thing to do when you've been ghosted
Is take him at his (lack of) word and assume he's dead.
So sad, so young, his whole life before him.
Went on that dratted app one day
Chatted you up, dated you once or twice
Had a kiss or even vigorous successful sex
Promised he'd call or text or date some more
And then, poor sausage, he just went and died!
Now he's wandering the hot halls of Hell
A pallid ghost of what might have been
If he wasn't such a fuckwit weasel ghost
Always looking for a new bright green
Elysian field to sport in - that is
Until his hair falls out, his waist just disappears
And no more lovely girls will glance his way
He's just a ghost, ex-personated, dead
Forget him and, while your sun is shining,
Find a true heart, and make that precious hay.

If Sir Thomas Wyatt were a woman today

They flee from me that sometimes did me swipe
Then with sock'd foot walked into my chamber.
I have seen them gentle, tame and meek
That now are wild and do not remember
That sometimes they put themselves in danger
To take pizza from my hand; and now they range
Busily seeking for continual change.

Thanked be fortune it has been otherwise
Twenty times better; but once so special,
With me in black lace knickers after pleasant guise,
And with my toes I hooked his Calvin Kleins to fall
And he me caught in his arms long and small;
Therewithall so deeply did me kiss
And softly said, "Do you like it like this?"

It was no dream: I lay broad waking.
But all is turned thorough my gentleness
Into a strange fashion of forsaking;
And I have leave to go of his ghostliness,
And he on Tinder to find newfangleness.
But since that I so kindly am served
I would fain to know what he hath deserved.

Sleeping beauty

A first kiss after 100 years,
Actually 31 since I met my fate,
And 5 since I'd fled
But not escaped.
By total happenstance,
A kiss against the wall of that first flat
Where married bliss within 3 weeks
Glitched and slid off track.
Alas my thorny bed was made
The cradle curse had bound me tight,
I didn't fight it, just strove
All the harder
Thinking that I'd failed at love.
Bills were red, car was trashed,
Our flat ransacked by junkies,
Up against the wall of which
I was being awoken
From spellbound sleep
By a textbook handsome prince.
He broke the spell and set me free.

Love flies

One evening long ago
When I was lit with love
Or was it lust?
The city seemed like paradise
To my dazzled eyes
I ran down Notting Hill
And took flight
Cleared a traffic boundary
With one bound
The witnesses
Could not believe their eyes
As, lacking in the sporting gene,
I seemed to fly that night.

Sparrow in my kitchen

Hot and beating in my hand
Tiny body wild with life
Fragile bones and legs like febrile sticks
Configured just like me
With beating heart, hot blood
And pentadactyl limbs
Hers to forge a path through air
Mine to grasp and hold
In my hot glove of bone and skin
Feathers thistledown against my palm

I brought the creature close
Against my eye so I could see
The little seeing eye look back
In terror at a monstrous me
Desiring only to set her free

Bluebirds

The blue-footed boobie
Is an engaging sea bird
Easily recognised by its blue feet.
My right boob is blue,
Instantly recognisable
As having been pumped with dye
And mined for cancer.
It is, in fact, a blue tit.

Might've been

I clocked your stubbled head online one day
Your lips were full and soft, your scalp quite bare
I liked your half-turned look and what you had to say

We took to chat and there we found a way
To get on well and flirt and talk and share
I clocked your stubbled head online one day

I held my virtual nose and jumped that day
In a mad dating world you were quite rare
I liked your half-turned look and what you had to say

We met in real life, but then you couldn't stay
Did other punters see an ill-matched pair?
I clocked your stubbled head online one day

You took me in your arms but then you went away
My quiet, neglected feelings had begun to stir
I liked your half-turned look and what you had to say

I sort of said I'd wait while you went on your way
Occam's razor tells me you've been eaten by a bear
I clocked your stubbled head online one day
I liked your half-turned look and what you had to say

Bearded lady

I haven't plucked my chin in months
On it grows a single hair
As a sideshow I would fail
To match the fairest bearded ladies
In their booths and corsets
Bonnets, buttons, boots and flounces
Silk stockings and enormous drawers.

I must arise and fetch my tweezers
Go on display post-lockdown
Beardless as a boy I hope.
Lipstick carefully applied
Eyelids painted, hair in curls
All ready for a fresh new world.

Dear teenage boy

When I was wholly
Institutionalised
By single-sex boarding school
From 7 years 3 months
To 17 years 9 months
I caught your eye
But I
Was habituated like a nun,
A teenager
Stuck like dinosaur DNA
In a blob of glistening amber
Bound, like feet
In the double bind
Of being female.
From your
Boys' boarding school,
You wrote:
'Getting
A letter from you
Is as good as a
Hot shower after hockey'.
Until this year
I had no idea
What you meant, so I spurned you
Embarrassed and uncomfortable,
Infected by parents
Whose early passion was replaced
By disgust, distrust, dislike.
You conjured your strong
Young naked male body
For me, shot with

Shards of boiling water.
I was frightened
Out of my virginal wits.
I had no map for loving masculinity
To help me understand
And enjoy your words.
Now as I take a shower
After every run each day
My body knows
What you were feeling.
I repeat your passionate
Teenage alliteration in my head
And apologise for
My stunted teenage self
Rejecting you.

On Kings Cross Station I

Went to Kings Cross Station.
Was a year since she had died.
Grief lay in wait on Platform 3
Where we'd held each other.
Me desperate, clinging, felt her fine bones
Within the hopeless circle of my arms.

Grief came at me like weather
Like a squall at sea from peerless blue
A sudden crack in time, a leak
To let through that which had been hidden
Unbound, a deluge, like a weapon
Invisible, scentless, undetectable
I suspected nothing till it hit.
A perfect ambush, neatly done.

In that moment I was wrenched,
Ripped, overwhelmed by grief.
Stepped into a wall of pain
My mouth fell open and I howled,
My face awash with tears and snot.
I could not move, grief held me
In its grip and shook me clean.

I do not know how long it took
World walked by embarrassed
By my disintegration in grief's embrace.
The British don't deal well with grief's raw face

Do not go dowdy

Do not go dowdy into that dark night
Style should not fade near close of play
Dance, sing, embrace the flying of the light

Wise women ignore the rules and take flight.
With early years consumed by work and young, they
Must not go dowdy into that dark night

Good women catch a wave in bright sunlight
Bikini-clad and plunging through the bay.
They dance, sing, embrace the flying light

Wild wanton women catch the joy in flight
Wear red satin - it's not too late to stray
And feed on honeydew before that last dark night

Bright girls, brave women, with deep insight
Their eyes not blinded by convention, they
Dance, sing, embrace the flying of the light

And you, my mother, now so far from sight
Bless me with your style, your grace, I pray
You did not go dowdy into that dark night
You joyfully embraced the flying of the light

Warm enough

On the scale of warm enough
To just that bit chilly,
Shivering, cramped and freezing,
Starved, which meant frozen
In a perishing distant past

There's a precise point when something
Triggers you to rise
And fetch your cardie from
Wherever you dropped it
When things equalised
Last time on the cold to comfort axis.

When I was starved some 20 years
Of mothering, my mother's cousin Jean
Said to me, 'Are you warm enough?' I cried.

It'd been a long time since
My being warm enough had
Been anyone's concern.

That's what being a grown up is.
You must make sure you're
Warm enough as everyone
Formerly interested has died.

Back to school

When I think of going back to school
Miss Wright is conjured in my mind
Stiff Sixties hair, curled up
A-line turquoise dress, winged glasses
Long pale fingernails tapping.
We had a playground chant
Based upon her mode of speech:
'How now, Edwina
Have you got your pencil?
I hope you've been excused.'

I'm still allergic to the sound of
Chilterns, Cheviots, Mendips,
Cotswolds, Malverns.
For some reason the Pennines
Don't bother me so much.
The other innocent English hills
Dump me straight back into
The exquisite boredom of
That long-lost September afternoon,
Dust hanging petrified in sunbeams
In those scruffy classrooms
Above the prep school stables.

When I was told my mother'd died
(I was 34 and a mum myself),
The first words that came to me were
'I don't want to go back to school
For the rest of my life.'
I was seven, you see,
When torn from her and sent away
To board and be profoundly bored.

Not neutrinos

I must let feelings
Flow through my body
Like solar neutrinos.
The likelihood of
Hitting a sore spot
Is infinitely higher
Than that of a neutrino colliding
With a proton or neutron
In our bodies.
Which is $1.77 \times 10^{(-20)}$ (to the negative power of 20).
Calculate length of life,
Factor in
Early separation
Sundry bullying
Numberless rejections
And
Not being loved × infinity
Means
Soft body stuffed
With sore spots.
Whereas, at a sub-atomic level, our bodies are
A fragile universe of sub-nuclear particles
Floating in almost infinite space,
We are echoing chambers of simply nothing at all
So
The calculation
Of feelings hitting sore spots is
Much less slight.
Average number of neutron collisions in your body per lifetime?
5,092
Infinite is the number of collisions

Between those inconvenient feelings
And invisible inflammation.
So
Allowing feelings to pass
Through ourselves
Is not like neutrinos at all.
More like being blasted with a 12-bore
Shotgun colandering flesh as the lead tears
Ragged, bloody passages.
And I should stop using this
Baseless neutrino simile
Right now.

Not drowning

I nearly drowned about four times
My head beneath the waves had sunk
The adults rescued me betimes
I nearly drowned about four times
I was submerged in subtle crimes
Debt's cesspit held me in its stink
I didn't drown that one last time
No adults came – I did not sink

Witches' recruitment drive

The last thing you should do in lockdown
Is follow recipes and bake some bread
You see it on screen coming from an oven
Fragrant, steaming, glistening and brown.
It's oh so tempting to join the throng
Of obsessive cake bakers and sourdough bores.
Better study witchs' recipes and join a coven
As dancing outdoors in the nude is preferable
To eating carbs and sitting still indoors
And no one wants to gobble tiny eyes and toes
Tongues and fur and leg and wing
Let alone the sting of anything.
Far better to compound a witchy hex
To blight our so-called leaders with an itch
(Now all our pleasures are illegal, even sex)
Than sit at home and stuff ourselves with cake.
The internet is messing with our heads
And bodies, friends. Choose an occult hobby
Lest we all emerge impersonating Mr Blobby.

Ladies beware

Never wed a man who hates his mother
Better wrestle with a spitting cobra

Either he's looking for another
Mother, perfect in every single way
Or he wants to take out all those feelings
Of jealousy, rejection and confusion

Either way it won't be healing
Without a miracle of transformation
And those are vanishingly rare

A man who hates his mother has
All the seed of patriarchy breeding
Justification in his hurting mind
His mother is to blame… or not

Women are not perfect after all
But wrong and careless deeds
Neglect, unkindness, spoiling, booze
Have planted seeds
That grow all rank and twisted through his life

It's not your fault he can't be kind
And you can never be his perfect wife

The new Narcissus

She's a mirror of water glass and tears.
Narcissus grabs her throat and shouts into her face.
You're fat and ugly, foolish thing of fears.
Her wet scared face reflects his own disgrace.
I'm nothing but a really lovely guy
I work so hard and take care of you all
You're wrong and I don't like it when you cry
You're just depressed, I hate it when you bawl
Why are you unhappy when I love you so
Only last week I brought you flowers and wine
His hand draws back, she flinches from the blow
'You can't escape, you'll always just be mine!'
She knows that only she can make this cease
No one's coming, she must sign her own release.

Arclight

Candlelight
Moonlight
Fairylights
Bedside light

Striplight
Nightlight
Fridge light
Oven light

Gaslight
Streetlight
Headlights
Torchlight

Darkness

In the British Museum

Was it for those girls
As for us before a teenage dance
Excited, brave, dressed in their best
Did they giggle over handsome soldiers
Chat and help each other weave those plaits
With golden leaves and wires
Rub scented oils on unlined necks
Brush kohl around their peerless eyes
Crush red petals
To bring a fragile blush
To cheeks that hidden fear had blanched
Did they believe
The party would go on beyond
The tomb's threshold.
Who spiked their drinks
To dull their fears enough
That they'd walk willing down to die
In stinking darkness
Had they heard the horses scream
As priests slaughtered them to draw
The dead king's chariots into hell
Could they smell the blood
Or was their faith so strong
That they could override the carnage.

Now they lie
In orderly rows, curled like foetuses
Legs bent, hands under cheeks
Slotted neatly, facing all one way
No struggle and no signs of pain
Although it's hard to tell

Some 4,000 years have passed
Since those girls had lives cut short
To satisfy some entitled greed
For the best of company
Beyond the grave

River run

Swept away
Seize at nothing as the river twists in spate
Washed downstream
Water ebbs and swirls
You pour into my mind
I want time to stop
Moor you to me
Tie you up
Rock gently on the tide
We spin away too fast
Towards a sea of you and me
Flotsam turns and tumbles in the flood
River rages, rips through me, through you
Runs away from both
Water stills and pools

On failing at the challenge of co-ordinated lingerie

Why do knickers linger on
When the matching bra has long since gone?

Carpe tempore

Times when I seize the moment
Are not those glories of love or death, birth or grief
You might think.
When I wake in the moment
I'm standing up on the Tube
Reading
Ah, here I am, I say to myself
Almost daily.
How many decades spent commuting
I do not know nor care
All melt into that one moment
Of standing on a train
Lost in the writer's mind
Present in my own.
Now, that moment is replaced
As my scant horizon's shrunk to home
It's putting on the kettle
That ties me to the conscious moment.
So British, mild and comforting
I make a cup of tea
Before arriving at my work
In the room next door

Fly

Why
Is always
Single fly
Keep me company
In my deserted room
Where from?
No rotting corpses here
Just me
I smell delicious
Not food
For munching maggots
Yet
It not malicious
Or inauspicious
Or even vicious
It innocent zoom
But
Good company it not
Sigh

Caddis fly larva

Staring through water
Wearing all I own as armour
Glued on for protection
Rockingham teapot on my head
My mother's mothy cardigan
Rotting ancient lace
Tangled all about my stumpy limbs
Bedizened with outdated brooches
Dropping stones of glass and paste
My case reflects the swimming moon
Safety wear for life alone
All the while I'm just
That maggot thing submerged
Or maybe pupating in my tiny castle
Undulating to create a flow
Of oxygenated water.
I'm completely stuck in
Larval state of god knows what
The caddis fly in youth might be
I tell myself
So much more exciting and creative
Than the hairy greyish adult form....
And yet it leaves its watery nest
And flies towards the light.

Iron man

He's a hard man to crack
From hazelnut head
To leaving home at 17
And never glancing back.

From fixed gear carbon bike
To rock hard six pack.
Narrow hipped, stony cold.
Determined, strange and bold.

In the night gloom she noticed
Her HRT patch
Stuck to his adamantine thigh.
She stifled a laugh and peeled it back.
Would he be woman-soft by morning?

As it turned out
Both rigid bike tires had detumesced
Overnight
Not a great success

The loneliest fetishist

Do you wear tights?

All women wear tights.

Not all. My ex hated them. That's why we split up.
Jeans all the time. I was so frustrated.
What denier and colour tights do you like?
I'm looking for a woman who likes tights.
It's a prerequisite for me. Is that weird?

I don't think so. I don't know though. Is it?

Possibly. But I like weird. Do you?
When did you last wear tights?

Friday I think.

The tights thing is everything to me.

You realise I'm a writer which means I might use this?

I like it that you're interested. Can I be your subject?

I must confess that you almost certainly will be.

I could perhaps convince you otherwise about tights?
Tights are gorgeous if they are the right ones.
Marks & Spencer do a fantastic 30 denier black pair.
Have you tried them?

I do buy tights in Marks & Spencer as the quality is good.

Have you ever been encased in tights?

What does that mean? Wearing them all over?
Crumbs. Where did that come from?

I've no idea. It developed in my early teens.

You like women to put several pairs of tights on at once?

Yes all over. Me too. Using 3 pairs.
It's an amazing feeling.
Would you like to try it?

No thank you very much.

Ha ha it's hardly that deviant.
Would you like to meet?
We would meet in Marks & Spencer's hosiery department.

That would be a new kind of date indeed for me.

Would you like to buy tights with me?

No one's asked me to do that before.
Buying tights is usually an AHEM solitary activity.
Do you go shopping for tights with random women on a regular basis?

No never ever it's just a fantasy I am expressing
But I desperately need the reality.
Never ever ever ever had what I really needed.

It all sounds rather sad and lonely and difficult.

Yes it is. I am sad about it.

Well, I think we'll leave it there. Sorry not to be able to help.

Thank you for your time.
If you'd like to meet, let me know....

Swipe left

Bibble bobble
Stomachs wobble
Ciggies burn
Turkey necks gobble
Men with blondes
And men with bikes
Pints of beer...
Is that a pike?
Downturned mouths
And grey complexions
Urgent words
To make connections
Sofa snuggles
Grammar struggles
Nostrils gape
And stream and bubble
Desperation leaks from screens
'I just want love!'
They seem to scream.
And yet among that sickly crew
There is the odd exception...
You

That sexy ghost of a dress

'Rather surprisingly
I have your lovely old black
Sleeveless linen frock here,'
Texts my nearly ex-husband.
'Left by our son.'

A dress my mother made
From a Calvin Klein pattern
For my trousseaux
Nearly 30 years ago
Curvaceous honeymoon frock
Worn with black strappy heels
Symbolic of sex and fertility
Hope for the future

Now it's gone and sent itself forwards
Through time
Into a space that no longer
Holds my heart or shape
And where I don't belong.
A message from a bottled past
Into an unguessed future
From which all love has fled.
Honeymoon long melted
Marriage nearly spent

He texts a picture of my dress
He's laid it on its back, on his bed,
He's kind of crimped the waist
With his hands.

'Must've been in his luggage
By mistake,' says my nearly ex-husband.
You're my baggage, I think
Not by mistake.

The black linen, now soft and faded,
Still moulds my undepleted curves
'This frock is an old friend,' he says.

Some people have imaginary friends...

I confess to an imaginary valet
He puts no strain on my wallet.
Each morning I ask for my bed tea
And, courtesy of last night's me,
The tray is all ready for action
I just have to find the traction
To get out of bed and descend
To the kitchen, where my tea blend
Of Welsh Earl Grey and Yorkshire Gold
Loose leaf of course and quite bold
In flavour for a morning's cup
(It suits me well and wakes me up)
Awaits with china and a glass tea pot
Kettle renders filtered water hot.
Cosy on, and back into bed I get
Once there, the lack of valet I forget.

Solitary spooling

My life is counted down
In dishwasher cycles
38 minutes, 2 hours 20.
Kegel machine programmes
15, 25, 45 minutes.
8-hour work shifts
Early or very late.
Time remaining in Kindle chapters.
Couch to 5k extending runs
One minute up to 30.
Binged episodes, 30, 60, 90.
4-minute egg timings.
Google map journeys
(Although I always get there faster).
My wayward washing machine
Is not bound by its promise of
30-minute washes
It goes spinning on and on long
After my interest in its cycles is gone.
My sleep is planned to last 8 hours.
I tell Alexa to 'sleep in 10 minutes'
And she does, stopping
Mid-sentence - I've Pavlov trained
Myself to drop off then.
FitBit measures light and deep
REM and restlessness by the minute too.

These deliberate intervals
Take me from conception
On Christmas Day 1957
Minute by minute towards an end

I cannot imagine.
Definitely not a heaven.
I hope it's decades off
I've got so much to do.

Armed and dangerous

You'd think I'd really know by now
How to dispose my limbs for sleep
But no, that awkward arm will not allow
Me to detach from body and fall deep
Into the arms of Morpheus, my fickle beau,
Where warm and breathing byres of sheep
Should catch me as I drift on down.

When waking, limbs are tools to keep
Us upright, functioning, they allow
All manner of actions we hold cheap.
But then at night when we desire to sleep
They turn on us, and are endowed
With superfluity. A tangled heap
Of sweaty knots; you'd think they owe
Us peace - should curl up like puppies,
Help us rest and let us go, but no
They are incorrigibly attention seeking

It's a race - will we slide into grateful sleep
Before they start their stealthy mission creep?

Runner beans

From the train I espy
Hope-filled allotments.
But the runner beans,
Ranked steep heaps
More than man-height,
Stir in the gloaming
Menace and approach
Rustling with intent
Will they break into a run
As the sun sinks?

Runaway

I don't like my smell when I've been running
Acrid, unfamiliar, like cheap scent
Or a new lover I don't quite take to
Because their smell provokes my discontent.
I don't smell like me when I've been running
Who is this Lycra jogging woman anyway?
She's new to me; she just won't leave
Looks like I'll have to get to know her as
We're destined to run on until the end
I can't just ghost her like I would a lover
Make my excuses, leave her trotting
Sadly down the towpath and away
While I slink home, sink back into my books
And reverse engineer my Couch to 5k.

Temptation

When you're at strict bootcamp
And the dulcet tinkle of the ice cream van
Pierces the fearful hollow of your ear
And you've confessed your lust
To the whole improving group
For bottomless receptacles
Of the very lowest sort of ice cream
Fraught with transfats, powdered whey
(A waste product of the cheese industry)
Bulking agents, various gels and pastes
Derived from seaweed, pigs and corn
Artificial flavours, colouring,
Its airy texture invented by Mrs Thatcher
In her food chemist days (for which
She is less famous now)
What oh what do you do?
Press palms to ears and ignore
Mr Frosty's chilling siren call.

In the bin

'You'd be so pretty if only you were thin,'
Said public school boys pretending to be kind.
Our bodies felt like objects and we couldn't win

If you weren't just bones, blonde hair and skin
You weren't attractive, but you mustn't mind
When they said that you'd be pretty if only you were thin

They thought that we should take it on the chin
Such excellent advice as love was far from blind
We were potential status symbols and just couldn't win

Any wobble from the norm and we'd be in the bin
No matter how good our grades, how keen our minds
The only thing that mattered was a body that was thin

'Does my bum look big in this?' was actually a thing,
We were conditioned to our bodies being maligned
We tried to shrink ourselves in order to be thin

The Seventies were deadly as we starved to fit in
With standards that were impossibly unkind
'You'd be so pretty if only you were thin,'
Said public school boys pretending to be kind.

Stink

I smelt a smell
It was not nice
I searched about
Without success
I smelled my socks
My shoes, my feet
But none was guilty
All were sweet
Finally I tracked it
Down, the guilty thing
It wasn't something
Trod and spread
But merely paper
Sad and smeared
With cheese remains
Forgotten in the bin.
Cheese like love is
So delicious when desired
And so unpleasant
Thrown carelessly away
When all desire has fled.

I will only like you if my nose does

I run through air
Laced with invisible ribbons
Some vile, some divine.
A whiff of something dead and rotting,
Fox shit, dog poo, hot day bins.
An unwashed cyclist
Trails his stinking banner.
Crushed leaves, clean earth
Mown grass and scorched mud
Fresh water like the smell
Of life itself
Crude florals of deodorant and Daz
The tiny scents of flowers
Musky balsam of wet tree bark.
Roses overblown, just this side of nice
Woodsmoke from the boats
A cigarette, skunk reek
Diesel fumes and tarmac,
Tang of wet concrete.
Stories for a sense so
Underused in humans and
Considered rather shocking
Animal, sexual and earthy,
Even in this age of so-called freedom
Sanitised, deodorised and much too clean.
I will only like you if my nose does.

Lost

When a dog's lost
His owners are advised
To leave a coat imbued
With their familiar funk
Upon the ground where
He last was seen.
In the morning
He'll be found
Curled up and waiting.

Drop your scented coat, lost love
Where last you left me lonely
And I'll sit and wait forever
Wondering where you've been.

Grief has no shore

Grief's a sea that never ends
There is no pebble shore on which its waves can break
No cliffs to batter, no salt swamps
Tender with mangrove to seep amongst
There's no one waving on the further shore
No welcome home, no nothing after certain deaths
But grief
In all its many moods and shades
It's how they live in us
Joy and anger, laughter and regret
We both remember and forget.
My mother, as she lay wide waking,
Said, 'Who are all those people?'
To an empty wall
There is that lovely fantasy of those
Who've 'gone before' - I don't subscribe.
She also called my name, I was not there
I cannot think of this without pain.
Love has been niggardly with me you see
I have been the beat of only one true heart
Now still.
I read a man fled from the damned disease
To his ancient father
Sailed an ocean in a tiny boat
As he could not fly
'I wanted to go home,' he said.
Lucky man, I thought
There's no way home for me
No end to grief's long sea.

A first son

She held my baby in her arms
He was extremely new and smelled
As babies do of newness
So fresh and human
Almost musky
She breathed him in and
From her spilled
The tale of her first child
We thought she had
Just three sons, one
Had died we knew
By his own hand.

She said quite slowly
As she held my son
That there had been a boy before
Her eldest, now a banker.

Her voice was even, calm and warm
Her first boy, born in India
While the world waged war
Played with a block of ice
They used to cool the train
Sucked his tiny fingers
Caught a dysentery
And died.

One small death among
Millions round the world
She hadn't thought to mention him
Before, but the soft weight

And scent of my small son
His seaweed arms and silken skin
Roused up her baby's ghost
Within her aching breast

And there he was, complete.
We all were quiet and sat with her
And mourned that one small life
So long ago, so loved, so lost
In time and space.

Naked as Eve exiled from the garden of Eden

From a boat of wood
In the sweet river Avon
Like swans we swam
Bang in the middle
Of Stratford
Then, bobbing with my best friend
Eating sandwiches
In the sunshine.
I was 11 or so
Wearing brothers' turquoise
Hand-me-down bathing trunks
Something wasn't right
My boy body was not
A boy's body any more
My nipples turned to silk
Something new there
Buds, pink and pliable
Not little brown badges.
I pulled my top back on
Over swim damp skin
And never took it off again

Antithesis

I hate the sea, it's full of bones and death
I hate the sound of laughter, cruel and out of place
I loathe the scent of flowers, they wither, rot and stink
I hate the moon, she's barren, full of holes
I hate the light of stars that reaches us as ghosts of things long dead
I hate the smell of new mown grass, it's just the scent of silent screaming
As with everything
To which we cling
Like drowning men
There's darkness in the light
That only makes it shine
More bright

1919/2020

I'm still surprised
He recognised me
In all that hurrying crowd.
In decorous hat
And spectacles steamed up
My lips and nose quite hid
Beneath the mask that
We must wear to stop
Transmission of the current plague.
Breaking all the hygiene regulations
For right and proper use
Of public transport destinations
In times of pestilence
He leant towards me
With clear intent.
Flurried with surprise I
Pulled up my mask to hide my eyes
And let him press his lips
Upon my lonely mouth.
It was the sweetest kiss
I think I ever felt
So unexpected
The scent and sense of him
Filling me, an empty vessel
Surplus woman
Unwanted and despised

A last Titanic menu

Back into their element
Tumbled oysters, plain and smoked sardines
Brill, anchovies, potted shrimps
Soused herring, chowder of clams
Followed by Virginia hams
And consommé Olga
Caviar from the Volga
Filet mignon and the roasted lamb
Cheshire, Stilton, Roquefort and Edam
Chicken Lyonnaise
And the salmon mayonnaise
Roast squab and cress
Loved passengers in evening dress
Orchestra and deck chairs
Chocolate and vanilla eclairs
Together with the finest wines
Bottles all are drowned in brine.
Traces of that menu now
Are 370 miles off Newfoundland
12,600 feet down.

Skin

I owe my face to good skincare
I learned it at my mother's knee
By candlelight it's still quite fair
I owe my face to good skincare
In natural light you see the bare
Truth of years of love and grief
I owe my face to good skincare
I learned it at my mother's knee

Kissing

Wasn't even my best nipple
In medical terms 'shy', Grade 2, inverted
Not all those hungry babies (5)
Let alone you as we flirted
Could leave it extroverted

Love is blind

Trouble with love is
It wraps about its object
Unearned riches of
Stitched-on seed pearls
Soft and silken pile
Fascinating byways
Words you've never heard before
Music that twines through the mind
Scents so rich and strange
They make you faint
Sunbeams piercing iron cumulus
Climbing to anvil heights
Tumbling pastures
Dotted with sheep
Like lice in electric hair
Woods at dawn wearing mist
Dropped like knickers around slim ankles

Glamour melts as magic fades
You're left with
Bobbled polyester
Wet tarmac culs-de sac
Clichés
Europop
Brut
Endless days dulled by flat grey skies
Scrubby dog-shit wasteland
Grass rank and bleached by dirty air
Beige Epiphany Christmas trees
Dumped in dying heaps

Love is blind
Time strips our minds
Takes Nitromors to glamour.
Lucky ones who find true love
Don't mind

Long after Sappho

Hesperus

Bright day scatters us until
Venus masquerading as the evening star
Calls us home as love should do
Sheep and goats wander to their fold
My child returns
And nestles by my side

Midnight

Moon has gone
Any moving star has left the sky
Midnight tips the sleeping hours
Towards another day
I slide my hand across the sheet
You are not there

Acknowledgements

Thank you to Paul Forster whose enthusiasm freed me to perform my poetry at *That's What She Said,* and the audiences who've clapped and laughed – you all gave me heart. Thank you to Bernardine Evaristo, my Brunel dissertation supervisor, whose feedback gave me joy, whose originality inspires me, and who pushed me to experiment with both verse and prose. Thank you to everyone who helped make *The Virtual Decameron 2020* a success by contributing, reading and commenting to help while away lockdown on Facebook. Thank you Maud Adderley and Maggie Alderson whose excellent judgement and virtual blue pencils were the editing I needed. Thanks to Archie Young, who improved my blurb - often the hardest thing to write. Thank you Christian Cuninghame without whom I don't think this slim volume would have happened. Thank you to Paula Rae Gibson, who created the wonderful cover art. Thank you to Sadie Butterworth-Jones for the cover design. Jordan Birch did the proof read - his main comment being: 'That's a myth about Margaret Thatcher by the way. Soft serve ice cream was invented when she was 14. I don't think that affects the artistic value of the poem though'.

Praise for fiction by Josa Keyes

One Apple Tasted

'Josa Young debuts with an entertaining and charming romance about love, sex and the upper-middle classes behaving badly.' The Independent

'Delicious froth combines with wit and insight in this romantic comedy of manners.' Marika Cobbold

'By far the best-written new romantic comedy I've read this year.' Amanda Craig

'Funny, warm, touchingly eccentric and irresistibly readable.' Julie Myerson

'Compelling, original, cleverly plotted and funny.' Isabel Wolff

'Smart, funny and bitter-sweet, Josa Young's debut is so well observed and so fresh that it stands out head and shoulders.' Elizabeth Buchan

Sail Upon the Land

'There are some sentences in it which are so beautiful, I read them again and again.' Maggie Alderson

'Love, love, love this book!' the Historical Novel Society

'A sweeping multi-generational tale that will catch your heart.' Katie Fforde

'Living characters and vivid locations, acute observations.' Charity Norman

'Her eye for period detail is masterly and her characters so vivid they dance off the page.' Rachel Hore

'Full of drama, pain, suffering, steadfastness and ultimately redemption.' Helen Walters

'There's something verging on magical about this book.' Ms_Rebecca on Goodreads

CPSIA information can be obtained
at www.ICGtesting.com
Printed in the USA
BVHW091317020621
608650BV00001B/208

9 780993 124853